SUPER SMART INFORMATION STRATEGIES

GO STRAIGHT TO THE SOURCE

by Kristin Fontichia

CHERRY LAKE PUBLISHING • ANN ARBOR, MICHIGAN

CHERRY LAKE
Publishing

Published in the United States of America
by Cherry Lake Publishing
Ann Arbor, Michigan
www.cherrylakepublishing.com

Content Adviser: Gail Dickinson, PhD, Associate Professor, Old Dominion University, Norfolk, Virginia

Book design and illustration: The Design Lab

Photo credits: Cover, ©Jacek Chabraszewski, used under license from Shutterstock, Inc.; pages 3, 13 top, 14 center, 14 right, and 18, ©iStockphoto.com/bluestocking; page 5, ©Andrew S., used under license from Shutterstock, Inc.; page 9, ©thatsmymop, used under license from Shutterstock, Inc.; page 11, ©Najin, used under license from Shutterstock, Inc.; page 13 bottom, ©Library of Congress, Prints & Photographs Division, LC-DIG-cwpb-04351; page 14 left, ©Elena Ray, used under license from Shutterstock, Inc.; page 15, ©dpaint, used under license from Shutterstock, Inc.; page 16, ©Keith Wheatley, used under license from Shutterstock, Inc.; page 19, ©The Field Museum, Neg#: GN90799d_JWH_006w; page 20, ©Doan, used under license from Shutterstock, Inc.; page 23, ©Library of Congress, Rare Book and Special Collections Division.; page 25, ©Lebrecht Music and Arts Photo Library/Alamy; page 28, ©Nancy Catherine Walker, used under license from Shutterstock, Inc.

Library of Congress Cataloging-in-Publication Data
Fontichiaro, Kristin.
 Super smart information strategies. Go straight to the source / by Kristin Fontichiaro.
 p. cm.—(Information explorer)
 Includes bibliographical references and index.
  ISBN-13: 978-1-60279-640-9 (lib.bdg.)
  ISBN-13: 978-1-61080-257-4 (pbk.)
 1. Information resources—Juvenile literature. 2. History—Sources—Juvenile literature. 3. Research—Juvenile literature.
 I. Title. II. Title: Go straight to the source. III. Series.
  ZA3070.F66 2010
  020—dc22
                                    2009028057

Cherry Lake Publishing would like to acknowledge the work of The Partnership for 21st Century Skills. Please visit www.21stcenturyskills.org for more information.

Printed in the United States of America
Corporate Graphics Inc.
September 2011
CLFA09

Table of Contents

4 Chapter One
Learning from Primary Sources

9 Chapter Two
A Picture Is Worth a Thousand Words

16 Chapter Three
If These Things Could Talk

21 Chapter Four
Words Can Teach

26 Chapter Five
Putting It All Together

30 Glossary
31 Find Out More
32 Index
32 About the Author

CHAPTER ONE

Learning from Primary Sources

Try to solve this research riddle: They're important. They're interesting. They make history come alive. What are they? Primary sources! Primary sources invite you into another world—the world of the topic you are studying.

What are primary sources? They are items or records that were created during a particular period in history. Common kinds of primary sources include objects or artifacts. Toys and clothing are artifacts. Images, such as photographs, are also primary sources. Documents are another type of primary source. The Declaration of Independence is a document. Newspapers are another kind of document. Birth certificates are more examples. So are blogs created by soldiers during a war. The important thing to keep in mind is that primary sources comes from witnesses to a period of time or event. These sources give us firsthand knowledge about life in other places and times.

What can you learn about people of the past by studying what they wore, bought, wrote, and read? What can you discover about an event by reading a

A passport is a primary source document. It is used when a person travels from one country to another. What could you learn from studying someone's passport?

speech or looking at an image? A lot! Primary sources help you dig deeper into history. That is what going straight to the source is all about.

You might think that all primary sources are old, such as a great-grandfather's birth certificate. But primary sources can be created anytime. Imagine that it's your birthday. A photo of the party would be an example of a primary source image. Your birthday presents are artifacts. An e-mail you send to a friend describing the party is a document. Those items all become primary sources about your party because a witness created them. Someone can study those sources to learn about your party.

TRY THIS!

Pretend an evening news program wants to do a story about you. The broadcast will discuss your hobbies, interests, and family. What kinds of primary sources could you provide to help the reporters paint a clear picture of who you are? Could you use photographs? How about your soccer or basketball uniform? Or a journal entry you would like to share? What would the images, objects, or documents reveal about you?

Report Card

Math	A+
Science	B-
Reading	B+
Social Studies	C+

If you become famous, the things you used as a child might be kept in a museum! These artifacts would help people learn more about you.

Let's say your social studies textbook discusses the War of 1812. Were the textbook's authors alive to witness the War of 1812? Of course not! That makes your textbook a secondary source. It was written by people who have studied history but weren't present to experience the events. Secondary sources describe historical periods or events. But they were created after those events occurred. Encyclopedia articles are secondary sources, too. Information explorers know that Web sites or encyclopedias are great for explaining topics. But they are not the only sources of important information. That's where primary sources come in handy.

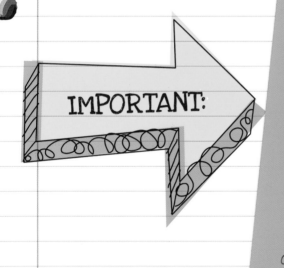

IMPORTANT:

Primary sources are amazing learning tools. But that doesn't mean you should ignore secondary sources. Both types of sources have their own strengths. A secondary source such as a good textbook or Web site can help you find out how experts have come to understand a historical period. It is a smart idea to use a combination of primary and secondary sources for research. You will have a better understanding of your topic.

TRY THIS!

Practice identifying sources. Which items in this list are primary sources? Which are secondary? Go a step further and also identify the type of source for each item. Is it an artifact, image, or document?

PRIMARY OR SECONDARY SOURCE?

1. Your report card from last year
2. A textbook about the American Civil War
3. A photograph taken by a photographer during the American Civil War
4. A student's history report about the American Civil War
5. A World War II rifle
6. An encyclopedia article about the Wright brothers
7. A photograph of the Wright brothers' first flight
8. A Web site created by a first grader about the Wright brothers
9. A letter from Orville Wright to Wilbur Wright
10. A map made by French explorers 200 years ago

Check your answers. How did you do?

Primary sources: 1 (document); 3 (image); 5 (artifact); 7 (image); 9 (document); 10 (image)

Secondary sources: 2 (document); 4 (document); 6 (document); 8 (document)

CHAPTER TWO
A Picture Is Worth a Thousand Words

You may think you can learn only by reading words. Not true! Images can give us powerful messages, too. A primary source image is any picture, drawing, or photograph created during the time or event you are investigating.

Let's say you are studying the life of Abraham Lincoln. Here are some primary source images that might tell you more about him:

- Civil War maps
- Political cartoons published in newspapers while Lincoln was president
- Photographs of Lincoln

Abraham Lincoln was one of the first politicians to be photographed.

You can find good images at museums or historical libraries. You can also turn to books, computer databases, or Web sites.

Sometimes, looking at an image gives us answers. Other times, we think of new questions to research. Do you have a printout of your image? You can write notes or questions in the margins. If not, you might want to find a photo analysis worksheet or guide online. You can find a link to one option at the back of this book. You can also take notes on a chart or blank piece of paper. Think in three steps as you study images: what you see, what you think it means, and what you wonder.

Start with what you see. Describe what is in the picture. Ask yourself these questions:

- What kind of image is this? A map, political cartoon, painting, sketch, or photograph?
- Are there words or dates on this image that give more information?
- What do you see in the foreground of the image? If there are people, how are they posed? What are they doing? What clothing are they wearing? What objects are they holding?
- What do you see in the background of the image? Buildings? Nature? Furniture?
- Does the image have a caption? What information does it provide?

Be careful about making assumptions. If there is a man, a woman, and two children in a photograph, write down "man, woman, two children" in your notes. You might want to write down "mother, father, sister, and brother." But think about it. Do you know for sure that they are related just by looking at the photograph? No. That is an assumption. They could be two teachers and two students! Later, you might use other clues in the photograph to decide that they are a family. This is called inferring.

How do these people know one another? We can't know for sure just by looking at this photograph.

Now consider what you think about the image. Dig deeper and think about what the image means. Ask yourself these questions:

- Who are the people in the image?
- Are there any symbols?
- What might those symbols mean? How do you know?
- Can you draw any conclusions or inferences from the observations you made earlier?

Don't forget to take into account what you wonder. You may discover that looking at the image makes you think of some new questions. List them. Your questions might lead your research in different directions.

Let's try analyzing an image. On the opposite page, there is a photo from the American Memory historical collections of the Library of Congress (shortcut URL: http://bit.ly/F8cWj). The Web site tells us that this is a Civil War photograph of Abraham Lincoln visiting Union general George B. McClellan.

As you can see, this photograph gives us a glimpse into an important time in history. But it also leaves us with questions. Why was a president at the scene? Why is a flag on the table? Who was General McClellan?

The information we discover and the questions we have keep us excited about doing research. Maybe a deeper investigation of Antietam would give us more answers. Keep going with your research!

Clothes on rack. Is rack made out of branches? How long has McClellan been at this site?

Cracks or folds in the image. How did it get damaged?

Tent. Tall ceiling! Why?

Man with beard in suit. It's Lincoln (the Web site said so, and I recognize him from other photos I've seen). Why is the president at a battlefield? Is he safe?

This must be General McClellan. What was his role in the Civil War? McClellan doesn't have a beard, so he must have shaved recently. Is this a staged photo? Photos took a long time. I think people had to stay still when photographed. They probably posed. Why?

Top hat is upside down. I think it is Lincoln's hat. Why is it upside down?

Pillow and quilt. Does the general sleep and work here? Is he meeting the president in his bedroom?

U.S. flag draped on table. Is it being used as a tablecloth? Why is it there?

Grass. It probably isn't winter. Web site says Fall 1862 during Battle of Antietam. Did the Union win this battle? Which side is currently winning the war?

Table. Looks like it might fold up for travel.

13

TRY THIS!

Test your image analysis muscles. Pick any historical period that interests you. The Roaring Twenties and World War II are two examples. Search for an interesting photograph taken during the era. Nonfiction books from your school or public library are good places to look. Search online, too. Make a photocopy or print out the image. Then study the image carefully. Are there people in the image? Who are they? How are the dressed? What are they doing? Are there objects? What are they? What can you learn or infer by studying the scene of the image? Take notes and write questions along the border of the image or on a separate sheet of paper. What do you see? Think? Wonder? You can use different colored pencils for each set of notes. Then research that period of time. What did you learn? Does it agree with your observations of the photograph?

Is a painting a primary source? Paintings can be considered primary sources. Studying paintings and the people who created them can teach us a lot. We can learn about changing styles, themes, and ways of thinking. What else can you discover by analyzing what is included—or left out—of a painting?

What questions do you have when you look at this painting?

CHAPTER THREE
If These Things Could Talk

Artifacts and objects are another kind of primary source. An ancient Greek vase is an artifact. So is your great-grandmother's cooking pot. Or a wedding dress.

You can find many images of artifacts online. As with images, think about what you see and what you wonder. But you will think about these ideas in different ways when studying artifacts.

Start by looking at the object and describing what you see. Ask yourself:

- What color is the object?
- What materials is it made of?
- What shape is it?
- What is its size?
- What condition is it in? Worn? Shiny? Cracked?

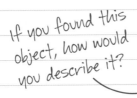

If you found this object, how would you describe it?

When you describe what you see, be careful to do just that: describe. Do not infer. Imagine that you have lost the object. How would you describe what it looks like? If you are examining an artifact in a museum or online, there may be a sign or caption that describes the object. That will give you extra clues and information.

Now think about the meaning of your observations. What do the clues tell you? For example:

1. Does the object seem fancy or simple? That might help you understand how much money the owner had.

2. Does the object look new or worn? This can help you determine if the object was used often.

3. Think about the 5 Ws (plus How) that reporters use to learn information:

   a. Who might have used the object?
   b. What was it used for?
   c. When was it used?
   d. Where was it used?
   e. Why was it used?
   f. How did you reach those conclusions?

Remember:
5 Ws + How

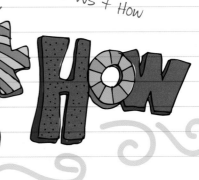

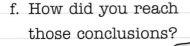

Are you still wondering anything about the object? Do you have new questions? Write them down. They can give you new research paths to follow.

Let's try studying an artifact. Did you know that the history of the Ferris wheel dates back more than 100 years? If you're lucky, you might be able to ride a modern version of one. But what if you wanted to study early models? One option is to look online for photos. The Commons on Flickr (www.flickr.com/commons) has many historical photographs from leading museums, archives, and libraries. On the opposite page is a photograph of the first Ferris wheel in the world—back in 1893! Notice the type of notes you might take as you study an image of this artifact.

When we look at the Ferris wheel, we discover some information. For example, we get a good idea of its size. But we are left with new questions. To answer those questions, you need to do some more research.

"See" items are red.
"Think" items are blue.
"Wonder" items are green.

18

Who invented this? How many people could ride in each car? How long did it take for the wheel to turn? How many times around were riders allowed to go? How much did it cost to build? When was it built? Was it ever taken down?

Look like train cars. Today's Ferris wheels often have benches. Why did they change?

I think it's amazing that this Ferris wheel dates back to 1893 (date is mentioned in caption on Web site).

What is the wheel made of? Metal?

This isn't a U.S. flag. What kind of flag is it?

Look how tiny the people seem! That helps me realize how enormous the Ferris wheel is.

The Ferris wheel is huge! How did people construct it? Did they build it here? Or build it somewhere else first? If so, where?

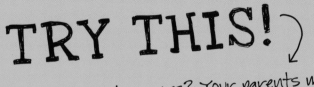

TRY THIS!

Do you love video games? Your parents may have liked them when they were younger, too. In fact, they may have used an Atari 2600 video game system. It was an early version of a home video game system. Ask your parents or other adults you trust. They might know someone who has saved an Atari system. Seeing one up close would be an excellent way to investigate. But you will probably have better luck finding a picture of one. Look in books about the history of video games. Or search online. After you've found a good image, study this Atari artifact carefully. Do you see controllers? Does the device look very advanced? Are there any game cartridges in the image as well? Take notes. What do you see? Think? Wonder?

← How is this controller like the one you use? How is it different?

CHAPTER FOUR
Words Can Teach

We learn from documents all the time. Newspaper articles, letters, and postcards are documents. So are blogs, e-mails, online chats, and instant messages. Advertisements, certificates, posters, and even paper money can all be primary source documents, too. When you look at text, think about the same three basic ideas: what you see, what you think, and what you wonder. Because you're working with words, you'll think about those three ideas in a different way.

Let's take a closer look at the words that make up primary sources.

Consider what you see or read. Keep these questions in mind:

- What do the words say?
- Are some words bigger or set in a different font? Those words are often important.
- If you find the document online, is there extra text or a caption that gives you more information?
- Are there images with the text? What do the images show?

Now focus on what you think. Try to answer these questions:

- Who is the audience?
- Who is the author or creator? Who is the person making the document for?
- What message is he or she sending?
- When was the message created?
- Where did this text appear? In a book? On a display?
- Why was the message made? To persuade? To inform? To sell something?
- How is the text arranged? Is that important? How do any images help get ideas across?

Finally, figure out what you wonder. What new questions do you have?

When you order at a restaurant, you look at the menu to see your options. The Library of Congress collects menus! This page from an 1866 menu came from the Ebbitt House in Washington, D.C. How were menus different back then? Let's look more closely as we analyze this document:

They use ½ when telling time. I think that 7 ½ means 7:30.

Fancy lettering for name of hotel. Does this mean it was expensive?

This document is a list of facts. I think that means that the purpose of the document was to inform. What do they serve? I would like to see a list of food.

Why is there no lunch? Why is dinner so early?

There is a separate section for nurses and children. There are different hours, too. They must not sit with their parents. Do they mean nurses as in hospital nurses? That sounds weird.

You can get lunch in your room. Why don't they serve it in the restaurant?

What is a Public Table? Why does it cost more if kids sat there?

This part of the menu looks like it was made to tell people when they should come to meals. It also gives some rules for the restaurant.

There is a safe. The owner doesn't get blamed if something is missing. Is the hotel unsafe? Why do people have to leave the key at the office?

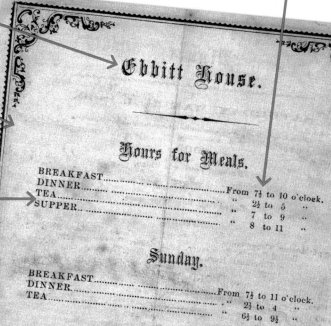

Ebbitt House.

Hours for Meals.

BREAKFAST	From 7½ to 10 o'clock.
DINNER	" 2½ to 5 "
TEA	" 7 to 9 "
SUPPER	" 8 to 11 "

Sunday.

BREAKFAST	From 7½ to 11 o'clock.
DINNER	" 2½ to 4 "
TEA	" 6½ to 9½ "

Nurses and Children's Table.

BREAKFAST	From 7 to 8 o'clock.
DINNER	" 12 to 1 "
TEA	" 6 to 7 "

NOTICE.

Guests having friends to dine will please give notice at the office. Meals, Lunches, or Fruit sent to Rooms, or carried from the table by guests will be charged extra.

Children occupying seats at the Public Table will be charged full price.

CAUTION.

Guests are respectfully informed that there is an Iron Safe in the Office, where all Money, Jewelry, or other valuables may be deposited, otherwise the Proprietor will not hold himself responsible for their loss. Upon leaving the room lock the door and leave the key at the office.

From reading this menu, we can see that children must have been treated differently in restaurants in the past!

TRY THIS!

Advertisements are everywhere. Television, radio, billboards, and magazines are a few places where we find ads. What can advertisements tell us about a culture or period of time? Find out! Look for a print ad from the past—the older, the better. You might want to look for ads for food products, objects, or clothing. Ask your teacher, librarian, or other adult to help you find one. You might find examples of historic ads in good nonfiction books about the history of advertising. You can also look online.

Look at the advertisement on page 25. Who seems to be the main audience for the ad? How does the company try to persuade the audience to buy the product or service? Take notes. Always keep in mind what you see, think, and wonder as you study these documents.

"Eat a Breakfast of Champions!"

SAY CHAMPIONS OF THE "BIG TOP"

ANTOINETTE CONCELLO
Antoinette Concello, audacious aerialiste, says: "A 'Breakfast of Champions'—a dish of Wheaties with plenty of milk or cream, sugar, and some kind of fruit, is 'tops' with most of the performers under the Big Top."

TIM McCOY
Col. Tim McCoy, Champion of the Range, says: "A big, heaping bowlful of Wheaties, with plenty of milk or cream, sugar, and some kind of fruit sure hits the spot. *That's a 'Breakfast of Champions.'* And that's the breakfast for me!"

JENNIE ROONEY
Jennie Rooney, of the daring "cloud swing" says: "I always include Wheaties among my carefully selected foods. Try Wheaties yourself, and see how good they are."

DOROTHY HERBERT
Dorothy Herbert, graceful and spirited horsewoman, says: "I advise wide awake girls who really want to do things, to keep in training. And eating a good big breakfast is part of my training program . . . Try Wheaties yourself. You'll say 'Wheaties are grand' too!"

Circus Champions . . . as well as champions in the world of sport—men like Joe DiMaggio, "Pepper" Martin, "Dixie" Howell . . . and others, agree: "Wheaties taste swell! Eat a 'Breakfast of Champions.

And a "Breakfast of Champions" is a big bowl of crispy, crunchy Wheaties, with plenty of milk or cream, sugar, and some kind of fruit.

Wheaties

Breakfast of Champions with plenty of milk or cream and some kind of fruit.

CHAPTER FIVE
Putting It All Together

When we research, we need to look at many sources. You might use a bunch of primary sources. But it's also a good idea to refer to secondary sources such as encyclopedias, articles from a database, and books. Take notes as you research. Then reread your notes. Think about how the information fits together like puzzle pieces to create a big picture. What have you learned? Do you have a good understanding of your topic? What if your notes don't agree or you still have questions? Do more research. That's what the pros do!

An encyclopedia isn't a primary source, but it is still a useful research tool!

TRY THIS!

Have you ever watched an adult empty his or her pockets or purse at the end of the day? Keys, receipts, a cell phone, wallet, and other items can help us learn more about him or her. Ask a parent or another adult you trust to participate in this activity. Have the adult take at least five things out of his or her pockets, wallet, or purse. Try to get at least one example each of an artifact, document, and image. Some sample items you might investigate include a grocery store receipt, a tube of lip balm, a ticket stub from a movie theater, or a wallet insert with photographs. Then, notebook in hand, study the items. Take notes about what you see, think, and wonder for each thing. Consider the items together. What can you learn about the person?

continued ⟶

What items would people find in your pockets?

Repeat the process with a friend. This time, study five things from his or her backpack. Can you put those primary sources together to learn more about your friend? Let's say you found a pair of reading glasses, two mystery novels, and two math tests with grades of "A+" on them. Maybe you'll discover that your friend wears glasses. Or loves to read. Or is very good at math. Have fun learning more about friends and family. Just remember to return the items to their owners!

What do you think you might learn about this boy by studying the items in his backpack?

You're now ready to use primary sources to answer questions and discover new ones. The activities in this book have helped you learn how to "read" images and artifacts, in addition to pieces of text. There are many kinds of primary source material. Have fun studying a variety of types. Here are some interesting options:

- Maps
- Political cartoons
- Audio material, including records, radio broadcasts, and podcasts
- Video material, including movies, documentaries, and video podcasts
- Interviews with witnesses

Going straight to the source and learning something new is like finding buried treasure. Great job, primary source detectives! You've learned to look at artifacts, documents, and images in different ways—through the eyes of an information explorer.

Congratulations! You are on your way to becoming an expert primary source detective.

Glossary

archives (AR-kivez) places where historical documents are
preserved

artifacts (ART-uh-faktss) objects made or changed by people

assumptions (uh-SUHMP-shuhnz) ideas or statements that are
not based on proven facts

documents (DOK-yuh-muhntss) text (on paper or saved electron-
ically) that gives information or proof of something

foreground (FOR-ground) the part of a picture that appears to be
nearest to the viewer

images (IM-i-jiz) pictures or other representations of a thing or
person

inferring (in-FUR-eeng) drawing a conclusion after studying the
facts

primary sources (PRYE-mair-ee SOR-siz) original documents,
objects, and other items that were created at the time being
studied and that come directly from witnesses to the event or
historical period

secondary source (SEK-uhn-der-ee SORSS) an account or record
of the past that was created after an event or historical period

symbols (SIM-buhlz) pictures or objects that represent something or remind people of something else; for example, the U.S.
flag is a symbol of the United States

witnesses (WIT-nis-iz) people who were present when an event
occurred or have personal knowledge of something

Find Out More

BOOKS

Hamilton, John. *Primary and Secondary Sources*. Edina, MN: ABDO
    Publishing Company, 2005.

Orr, Tamra B. *Extraordinary Research Projects*. New York: Franklin
    Watts, 2006.

Tait, Leia. *Primary Sources*. New York: Weigl Publishers, 2008.

WEB SITES

The Library of Congress—Questions for Analyzing Primary Sources

memory.loc.gov/learn/lessons/psources/studqsts.html

Look here for important points to keep in mind when evaluating primary sources.

Smithsonian Institution

www.si.edu/

Find photographs of artifacts and documents from throughout world history.

The U.S. National Archives and Records Administration—Photo Analysis Worksheet

www.archives.gov/education/lessons/worksheets/photo.html

Analyzing a primary source photograph? Use this helpful chart to organize your thoughts and observations.

Index

advertisements, 21, 24, 25
archives, 18
artifacts, 4, 5, 8, 16–18, 20, 27, 28, 29
audio, 29

birth certificates, 4, 5
blogs, 4, 21
books, 7, 8, 10, 14, 20, 22, 24, 26

captions, 10, 17, 19, 22
cartoons, 9, 10, 29
certificates, 4, 5, 21

databases, 10, 26
documents, 4, 5, 6, 8, 21–22, 23, 24, 27, 28, 29

e-mails, 5, 21
encyclopedias, 7, 8, 26

experts, 7

images, 4, 5, 6, 8, 9–12, 13, 14, 15, 16, 18, 19, 20, 22, 27, 29
inferring, 11, 12, 14, 17
instant messages, 21
interviews, 29

letters, 8, 21
libraries, 10, 14
Library of Congress, 12, 13, 22, 23

maps, 8, 9, 10, 29
museums, 10, 17, 18

newspapers, 4, 9, 21
notes, 10, 11, 13, 14, 18, 20, 24, 26, 27

objects, 4, 6, 10, 14, 16–18, 24
online chats, 21

online resources, 10, 14, 16, 17, 18, 20, 22, 24

postcards, 21
posters, 21
primary sources, 4–5, 6, 7, 8, 9, 13, 15, 16, 21, 26, 27–28, 29

questions, 10, 12, 14, 16, 17, 18, 22, 26, 29

secondary sources, 7, 8, 26
speeches, 5

textbooks, 7, 8

video, 29

Web sites, 7, 8, 10, 12, 13, 18, 19, 24
witnesses, 4, 5, 29

About the Author

Kristin Fontichiaro is an elementary school librarian for Birmingham Public Schools in Michigan. She is also an adjunct lecturer for the University of Michigan School of Information. She has written several books for teachers and librarians. This is her first book for children.